Pebble® Plus

Hands-On Science Fun

How to Make a
MYSTERY SMELL
BALLOON

Revised Edition

Lori Shores

Raintree is an imprint of Capstone Global Library Limited, a company incorporated in England and Wales having its registered office at 264 Banbury Road, Oxford, OX2 7DY – Registered company number: 6695582

www.raintree.co.uk
myorders@raintree.co.uk

Edited by Marissa Kirkman
Designed by Sarah Bennett
Picture research by Tracy Cummins
Production by Tori Abraham
Originated by Capstone Global Library Limited

ISBN 978 1 4747 5676 1
22 21 20 19 18
10 9 8 7 6 5 4 3 2 1

British Library Cataloging in Publication Data
A full catalogue record for this book is available from the British Library.

Printed and bound in India

Acknowledgements
We would like to thank the following for permission to reproduce photographs: Capstone Studio: Karon Dubke, Cover, 4, 5, 7, 9, 11, 12, 13, 15, 17, 19, 21, 22; Shutterstock: corbac40, Cover Design Element

The author would like to thank Dr Ronald Browne for his invaluable help in the preparation of this book.

Every effort has been made to contact copyright holders of material reproduced in this book. Any omissions will be rectified in subsequent printings if notice is given to the publisher.

All the Internet addresses (URLs) given in this book were valid at the time of going to press. However, due to the dynamic nature of the Internet, some addresses may have changed, or sites may have changed or ceased to exist since publication. While the author and publisher regret any inconvenience this may cause readers, no responsibility for any such changes can be accepted by either the author or the publisher.

Note to parents and teachers

The Hands-On Science Fun set supports National Curriculum requirements for science related to physical science. This book describes and illustrates making a mystery smell balloon. The images support early readers in understanding the text. The repetition of words and phrases helps early readers learn new words. This book also introduces early readers to subject-specific vocabulary words, which are defined in the Glossary section. Early readers may need assistance to read some words and to use the Contents, Glossary, Read more, Websites, Comprehension questions and Index sections of the book.

Contents

Safety note:
Please ask an adult to help you make
your mystery smell balloon.

Getting started

What's that smell?

Only you will know that

it's a mystery smell balloon.

Your friends won't believe

their noses!

What you need:

1 latex balloon

fork

1 clove of garlic

ribbon
or string

small funnel

Other smells to try:

5 mL vanilla extract
crushed onion

Making the secret smell

Peel the skin off
the clove of garlic.

Crush the clove with the fork.
The garlic will be squashed
and juicy.

Slide the small end of
the funnel into the opening
of the balloon.

Carefully push the wet garlic
down the funnel.

Next, blow up the balloon
as big as you can.

Tie the end of the balloon
and shake it around.

Sneak into a crowded room.
Tie the balloon to a chair
or door handle using a ribbon.

Now watch as your friends
notice the smell!

How does it work?

Smelly things give off

tiny pieces called molecules.

They are too small to see.

You smell garlic when

the molecules reach your nose.

Garlic molecules

pass through tiny holes

in the wall of the balloon.

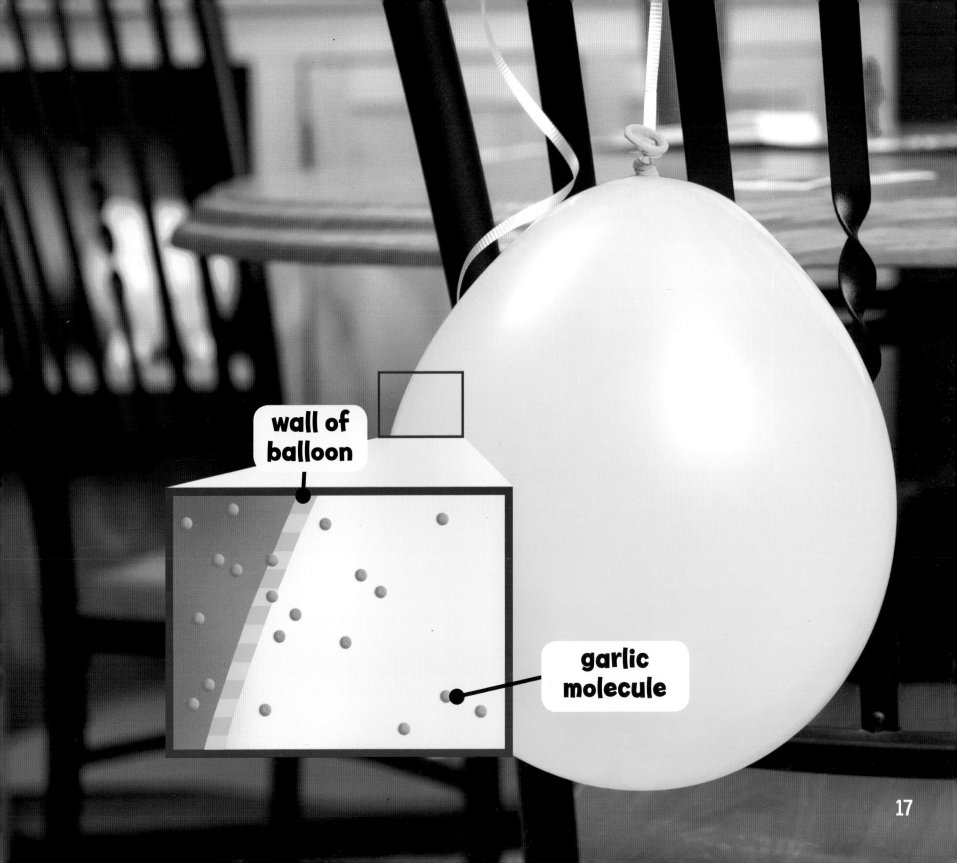

wall of balloon

garlic molecule

Air molecules are bigger.
They can't pass through
the holes as easily.
Air stays in the balloon longer
than the garlic molecules.

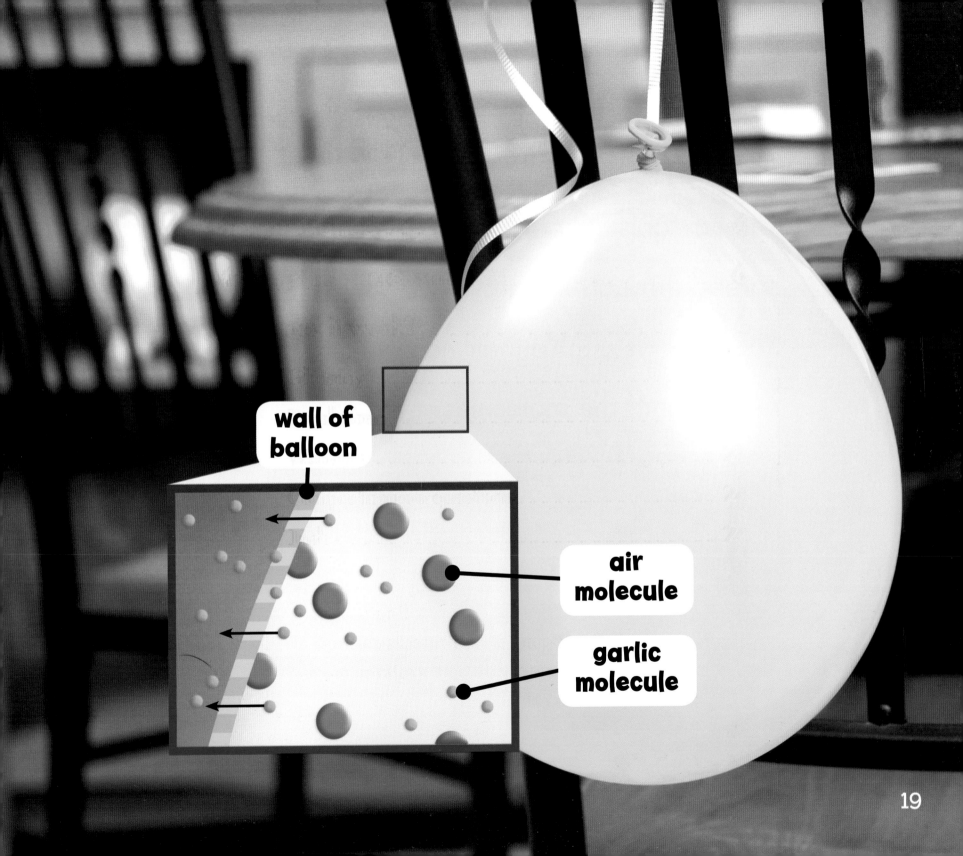

wall of
balloon

air
molecule

garlic
molecule

The tiny garlic molecules

spread through the air.

Your friends crinkle their noses

as they sniff the molecules.

Glossary

clove   one of the sections of a bulb of garlic

crinkle   wrinkle up

funnel   open cone that narrows to a tube

molecule   smallest part of an element that can exist and still keep the characteristics of the element

peel   remove the outer skin

Read more

Experiments in Material and Matter with Toys and Everyday Stuff (Fun Everyday Science Activities), Natalie Rompella (Raintree, 2015)

Mind-blowing Physical Science Activities (Curious Scientists), Rani Iyer (Raintree, 2017)

Science (Jobs If You Like…), Charlotte Guillain (Raintree, 2013)

Websites

www.bbc.co.uk/terrificscientific/curations/z22qtv4
Explore and contribute to real scientific investigations on the BBC's Terrific Science website.

www.bigeyedowl.co.uk/science/index.htm
Ideas to encourage and extend scientific skills.

www.science-sparks.com/category/early-years-science-2/sensorymessy-play/
More fun activity ideas to help investigate core science concepts.

Comprehension questions

1. How does the secret smell get inside of the balloon?

2. How does the smell get out of the balloon?

3. Describe why air molecules don't pass through the balloon as quickly as other molecules.

Index